# The Lost Diary of Queen Victoria's Undermaid

**Found by Alex Parsons**

**Illustrated by George Hollingworth**

Collins
An imprint of HarperCollins*Publishers*

First published in Great Britain by Collins in 1998
Collins is an imprint of HarperCollins*Publishers* Ltd
77-85 Fulham Palace Road, Hammersmith, London, W6 8JB

3 5 7 9 9 8 6 4 2

ISBN 0 00 694581-3

Printed and bound in Great Britain
by Caledonian International Book Manufacturing Ltd,
Glasgow G64

# MESSAGE TO READERS

The diaries of Mrs Flora Porter, née Flossie Ramsbotham, were found beneath the floorboards at Hampton Court Palace, during recent building works. The little notebooks were tied with pink ribbon and wrapped in a pair of red tartan knickerbockers. Whilst the knickerbockers were graciously received on behalf of the nation by the Victoria and Albert Museum, the diaries themselves met with nothing but scorn. The eminent historian, Professor Dullas Ditchwater (author of dozens of long and extremely dusty volumes about Queen Victoria) dismissed Flora's diaries as 'worthless gossip' and 'scandalous tittle-tattle'.

When Professor Ditchwater lobbed Flora's diaries out of his window, they fell into the hands of Alex Parsons, a not-so-eminent or expert historian. She immediately realised that important issues were revealed in the diaries, namely that even Kings and Queens wear underpants, and someone has to wash them. Now, thanks to Ms Parsons' timely catch, you too can view Queen Victoria's life and times from the unique perspective of the wash tub.

*January 1st, 1837*
*Snobby Manor, Snootyshire.*

'Do not forget, gentle reader, that servants are also human beings', it says in this book of Household Management I dug out of Lady Snobby's library. Oh yeah! That'll come as news to Lady La-di-dah Bossy Boots. Since when do I have time to be a human being, I'd like to know? Sixteen hours a day up to my elbows in soap suds, and life not made easier with the wretched butler trying to kiss me. (I wouldn't mind so much but he's got a wart on the end of his nose with three wiry hairs sticking out of it, yeeuch!) Miserable wages, miserable household, and the Snobbies are unbearable. Flossie Ramsbotham, you were born for better things.

Since this is the day to make New Year's resolutions here are mine:

1 Change my name. Flora McTavish sounds suitably romantic
2 Remember to wash behind my ears.
3 Forge a fantastic reference from Lady Snobby
4 Keep a diary for the rest of my life.
5 Apply for a job at Buckingham Palace.
6 Stop wiping my nose on my sleeve.

That should do it, I reckon.

# *Spring 1837*
# *Buckingham Palace*

Made it! What can one say about my new boss, our esteemed monarch, William one-vee? Well, to put it kindly, our dear King looks about a hundred years old and his eyes stick out like a frog's. He has zillions of children by an actress called Mrs Jordan and none at all by his wife, the rather dotty Queen Adelaide. Setting an example to the lower orders indeed!

WILLIAM IV AND PRINCESS VICTORIA

The heir to the throne of England is his niece, Princess Victoria, who lives with her pushy mama in Kensington Palace. Princess Victoria is exactly the same age as me *and* she keeps a diary. I think this is an omen.

Meanwhile down at the palace laundry I get to wash the king's drawers. They are not a pretty sight. He has three hundred pairs of fine linen underpants with holes in the front so he doesn't have to take all his clothes off when he goes for a piddle. The Queen has the same number of roomy drawers, trimmed with pintucks and lace.

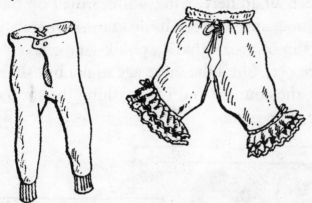

As everybody knows, ladies' drawers are not stitched together, otherwise we'd have to rummage about in an unseemly way under layers of petticoats every time nature called.

The head laundry maid told me that pants were named after a Christian martyr called Saint Pantalone. I have to take an interest in these things or I'd go mad.

## Summer 1837
## Buckingham Palace

It's been all go here. King William died on the 20th June, and now we have a new monarch. A mere slip of a girl (that's a polite way of saying she's short). She's the same age as me but she's ruling the country and I'm washing the sheets. There is no justice.

All the talk in the servants' hall is who the young Queen will marry. To my mind she seems a little over-friendly with Lord Melbourne, her Prime Minister, in spite of the fact he's as old as the hills. According to the underfootman, he's had a lot to put up with in his life. His wife, Lady Caroline Lamb, was completely unhinged and got up to all kinds of wild things with a very naughty poet called Lord Byron. The under-footman was trying to demonstrate some of the wilder things to me, when the housekeeper came in. She was not convinced that we were only playing at being Lord Byron and Lady Lamb, thus demonstrating our loyalty to Lord Melbourne.

I have been told to watch my step. The underfootman is called Brian and he is very handsome.

## 28th June, 1838
## Buckingham Palace

What a day! The gun salutes started at 4am and no one's had a wink of sleep since. Today the Queen was crowned in Westminster Abbey. It has been a wonderful day, the whole of the country has taken the young Queen to their hearts. Not surprising, considering what our last three kings were like. Sir Somebody Something described them as 'an imbecile, a profligate and a buffoon'. I've asked around and apparently that means a madman, a ladies' man, and a fool. Why don't people say what they mean?

BEFORE

THREE FOOLISH KINGS

AFTER

ONE WISE QUEEN

Apparently the Coronation didn't go quite as smoothly as planned, and that's probably because nobody planned it. Nobody understood the long, boring service and no-one noticed when the Archbishop turned over two pages at once.

All the Lords of the Realm had to go up to the Queen and kiss her hand. Lord Rolle, who is eighty-two and very frail, tottered up the altar steps, overbalanced with the weight of his robes, and fell over backwards. It's a day he'll not forget in a hurry!

A couple of the Lords started in on the champagne and cucumber sandwiches before the ceremony was over and were seen staggering about with their coronets over their noses and their stockings wrinkled round their ankles. One day, someone's going to invent stockings that stay up, just you wait and see.

After the Coronation celebrations were over, the new Queen rushed up the stairs to her room in the Palace to give her little spaniel, Dash, a bath. There's no telling how excitement takes people, is there? I think, if I'd just been crowned Queen, I'd be bathing in milk, swigging down the champers and inviting all my friends over to party, party, party.

# Winter 1838
## Buckingham Palace

After all the excitement, life goes on. I don't get to see much of Queen Vic, actually. She doesn't visit the laundry and I'm not exactly invited to tea in the Grand Saloon. Most of what I know I get from QV's Maids of the Bedchamber when they bring me the hampers of dirty linen to scrub. It's the gossip – and Brian the underfootman – that keeps me going. Take this week for instance. QV is *not* having a good time.

She's got a problem with her mother, the Duchess, who is plotting behind her daughter's back to be the power behind the throne, along with her 'financial adviser' (ho ho) Sir John Conroy. QV has started a rumour that Sir John is having an affair with one of the Ladies in Waiting. So you can imagine the atmosphere at the dinner table.

She's got a problem with her relations, who all turn out to be kings of Holland and Belgium and other such places, and all want favours from her while they fight with each other.

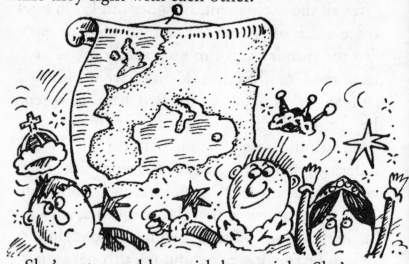

She's got a problem with her weight. She's getting distinctly plump and being so short, it shows. Her drawers are a size larger than they used to be. I should know. Lord M is trying to get her to take some exercise, but she says she won't and queens don't do what they don't want to do. She may live to regret this.

She's got an even bigger problem with Lord Melbourne. The thing is she's so dependent on him. She thinks everybody at the Palace (apart from Lord M and her beloved Baroness Lehzen – her old governess) are deaf, stupid and vulgar bores. She may be right of course, but what's going to happen to her when Lord M's party gets voted out of office? I think she can see it coming and it's making her sulky and lazy. Apparently she's even given up brushing her teeth.

## January 1839
## Buckingham Palace

What strange ideas some people have. The Queen's doctor is mad about fresh air, but just opening the windows doesn't seem to be enough for him, oh no! Dr. Clark wants to build a machine to pump air into Buckingham Palace because he thinks the corridors are clogged up with moisture from the trees in the back garden. He may be right – it is very stuffy here, especially in the laundry.

# March 1839
# Buckingham Palace

Well, finally there's a bit of life around the place. Some of QV's cousins have come on a visit, and for the first time in ages QV has got people of her own age to be with. I think she's rather taken with Prince Albert of Saxe Coburg, who is

actually quite handsome (but not as handsome as Brian).

Prince Albert & Victoria

A Post Script to the Great Buckingham Palace Ventilation Debate. A friend of Dr Clark's was due to come up with a new health and hygiene plan for the Palace, until someone read his latest book

Brian

and realised that Dr Arnott was off with the fairies. Apparently he believes we could all live to be 300 years old if we breathed enough fresh air. I'd like to give it a try!

# Spring 1839
## Buckingham Palace

Just as I thought. QV's in a real tizzy about losing Lord Melbourne and she's taken against the man who's due to be the next Prime Minister. According to her, Robert Peel minces about, shuffles his feet and points his toes. But is this a hanging offence? Is it not possible to govern a country whilst pointing one's toes?

The only bright side of it (as far as she's concerned) is that all the fretting about his mincing has made her a little less porky, so I've got a busy week ahead of me taking tucks in her drawers.

## *Autumn 1839*
## *Buckingham Palace*

Well, did I or did I not predict that QV had her eye on Prince Albert? He'd only been here five days when she started laughing too loudly, shaking her ringlets and generally going weak at the knees. He seems utterly taken with her, too (maybe she's started brushing her teeth again). QV didn't waste any time proposing to Albert, because that's the way queens do things.

I mentioned this to Brian but he has not taken the hint.

I finished a little early in the laundry last night, and got roped in by the scullery maid to help her peel apples. They've got this absurd apple-peeler. You're supposed to stick an apple in the bracket and turn the handle – so the blade follows the shape of the apple, occasionally gouging out pieces of skin. It would be quicker to peel them by hand, but they're gadget mad in the kitchen and there's no talking sense to them.

One day, someone will invent a machine for washing clothes, I just know it. But I am not holding my breath.

## January 1840
## Buckingham Palace

Nothing's simple when you're Queen. Not only did QV have to propose to Albert, instead of the other way round, she's now busy trying to sort out his title and the amount of money he's going to get. All very undignified, if you ask me.

I said to Brian, as I was scrubbing out the wash tubs: "Aren't we fortunate in being so ordinary that if we wanted to get married we could just go ahead without having to worry about who's got the grander title?"

Brian said: "You'll have to scrub a bit harder if you want to finish them tubs before midnight."

Will Brian turn out to be the romantic hero of my dreams? Will Brian's grammar improve? I am beginning to have doubts.

## February 10th, 1840
## Buckingham Palace

QV got married today. We've been working like slaves for weeks to make the day go smoothly.

First, Prince Albert sends his valet (blond hair, blue twinkly eyes, good strong legs) over from Saxe Coburg, or wherever he lives, with a dog called Eos. What they don't realise is that dogs equal dog hairs and slobbery chops so the bottom line is more washing.

Then comes Prince Albert (even more washing), then the wedding guests (more washing than ever before).

I was almost too exhausted to notice that QV looked quite pretty in her white silk dress, I only noticed that her lovely clean petticoats were brushing on the dusty ground and I said to my fellow laundry maid, Lucy, as we tumbled wearily into bed: "More bloomin' washing." Actually, I didn't say that, I said: "I rather fancy Albert's valet," and she said, "Join the queue."

## 10 June, 1840
## Buckingham Palace

Well, I hardly know where to begin. First things first though. The valet's a dead loss. He doesn't speak a word of English and spends far too much time admiring himself in mirrors. But Stanley, one of the new grooms at Windsor, is an absolute dish. He smiled at me once last week, and twice this week. That's what I call progress.

What else has happened? Ah yes, the Queen is pregnant (more washing to come) and Albert is getting all agitated about not having enough influence over the Queen like a proper husband should, but what can he expect? The wretched man has married the Queen of England, for goodness' sake.

Oh, I almost forgot. Some madman took a pot-shot at QV this evening, as she set out for a drive. Perhaps it is not as much fun being Queen as one might think.

But it is not much fun being a laundry maid either. While QV makes history, I make soap suds.

• First I have to sort the clothes. Lacy drawers and petticoats in one pile, chemises and cotton breeches in another.

• Then I fill the washtubs with hot soapy water.

• Then I scrub the cottons on a board, then the lacy bits.

• Then I put the clothes into another tub and pour boiling water over them.

• Then I add soap, put on the lid and dream about Stanley for half an hour while the clothes soak.

• Then I tip them out, drain them and rinse them in clean water in yet *another* tub.

• Then I wring out the clothes, using a mangle.

• Then I hang them out to dry.

• Then I start all over again.

Could Stanley love a woman with rough, red washtub hands?

## November 1840

I have to spend the winter in the laundry at Buckingham Palace, while Stanley is miles away, working in the stables at Windsor. This makes our romance quite difficult, but luckily, the British Post Office has come to our aid. They have just invented a penny post system, so I can buy a stamp for just one penny and send a letter to Stanley with SWALK on the back. He wasn't very keen on getting letters from me before, because under the old system he had to pay to *receive* a letter. Will he write back? I'm in such a tizz that I put too much starch in the Queen's drawers and the wardrobe maid was furious!

## December 1840

Oh the excitement! We had an intruder in the Palace! A little boy called Jones apparently crept in past all the footmen (I'm not surprised he crept past Brian, Brian notices NOTHING) and into the Queen's quarters. Lehzen, the Queen's old governess, actually discovered the lad hiding behind a sofa. Albert was livid. He said it was because of the sloppy security and a disorganised household, but then he's German and probably doesn't appreciate our easy-going British ways.

## July 1841
## Buckingham Palace

Lord Melbourne finally got his comeuppance in the elections, and we now have a new Prime Minister cluttering up the corridors and demanding lunch at all hours. Sir Robert Peel has been responsible for creating the police force and making them wear funny hats. But QV still hankers after Lord Melbourne and, so they say, Lord M pines for her attention.

I know all about pining, that nasty boy Stanley never replied to my letters. The household is moving to Windsor for the summer so I'll have plenty of opportunities to make him suffer for it.

## August 1841
## Windsor Castle

From my point of view, the problem with Windsor is that the windows don't fit in the kitchen, the oven doors don't close properly and the washtubs have splinters. But it doesn't seem to be anyone's job to fix these things.

The other problem is Stanley. He's been made head groom and now thinks he's all high and mighty and much too important for a lowly scrubber from the laundry. My heart is broken.

From QV's point of view the problem with Windsor is her subjects. Every time she sets off on a family walk in the park she bumps into crowds of curious subjects. I think she should look for a place tucked away in the country, miles from anywhere. I could go with her and sob into my washtub.

## January 1842
## Buckingham Palace

Our easy-going British ways are really getting up Albert's nose now. Actually it's Lehzen who manages the household and, quite frankly, she couldn't organise a pillow fight in a cushion factory. So with much weeping and wringing of hands, QV's agreed to get rid of her old governess and let Albert reorganise the place a bit. This should be *really* interesting.

If anyone had asked me, I could have told them why the household is in chaos. It's because no one's in charge and there's no co-ordination between departments. The Lord Steward's department lays the fires, but the Lord Chamberlain's department lights them. The result is that if the man who lights the fires does his rounds before the man who lays the fires, no fires get lit.

The Department of Woods and Forests cleans the outside of the windows, and the Lord Chamberlain's mob cleans the insides, but never at the same time. The result is that one side's always filthy.

Albert is charging round making lists and he's upsetting people left, right and centre.

## December 1842
## Windsor Castle

Well, I'll say this for Albert, when he gets going, he doesn't stop. You wouldn't believe what's been going on! I've been made Head Laundress: I've got brand new washtubs, a magnificent mangle, three assistants, a set of brand new irons and a Castle-wide system of laundry baskets. I am queen of all I survey, all I need now is a king.

Albert has some funny ideas about Christmas. Actually, it is all very jolly. He sent to Coburg for these fir trees and they're planted in tubs inside the Castle, with bright, sparkly decorations on them. He calls them *tanenbaum,* which, I'm told, means Christmas trees. Then he set up this table full of presents for the children and now he's out there pulling sledges and building snowmen and skating on the pond. In the evenings they play blind-man's buff and card games. Oh, how the other half live!

William Porter, a new underfootman, has taught me a wonderful new dance from Czechoslovakia called the Polka. We whirled round and round in each other's arms late into the night, past all those disapproving busts in the long corridor at Windsor. I am in love.

## January 1843
## Buckingham Palace

Oh, the stories that William can tell! He was with QV and Albert when they took their first train ride from Windsor to Paddington last year. William sounds wonderful... sorry I mean trains sound wonderful. Apparently, the train had to rattle along at breakneck speed because every time they slowed down a great crowd would gather beside the track. It's a bother for the Royals, really, all those people gawping at them. And what do they expect to see? They're just a rather ordinary-looking family, out of touch with the rest of us mortals. I should know they're ordinary, I wash their underwear.

## May 1843

Whatever will they think of next? As if cigars weren't disgusting enough, in France they have started shredding up tobacco leaves and rolling them in tissue paper – and guess what they're going to call them? Cigar-ettes! *Ooh la la*! They'll never catch on.

## Summer 1845

That little place in the country I was suggesting right back when Stanley nearly broke my heart, has turned out to be Osborne House, on the Isle of Wight. QV and Albert are planning to buy up half the island, to give them privacy. I hear that Albert is already drawing up building plans to turn the house from a modest home into a grand Italian villa. That man cannot leave anything alone.

## Autumn 1845

Another little titbit from the lips of my beloved fiancé, William. (I've been so excited about getting engaged that I have neglected my diary) QV and Albert were touring in Germany, but the people did not take to her. Of course, we're completely used to her serious little face, (or her pudgy pout if you don't mind risking being hung for treason) but the German people like to know if you're having fun, so Albert's been giving her smiling lessons.

## Winter 1845

The British press are actually beginning to notice the difference in life style between the squalor of the poor and the luxury (for some) at the Palace. Sir Robert Peel is doing his best to explain this to his Sovereign. Two men came to the Palace with a petition for Prince Albert. They requested that he and QV should wear short trousers and petticoats to help the British silk and stocking industry. Were they *serious*? Can they imagine how ridiculous that would look?

## Summer 1846
## Osborne House

There are builders everywhere. That's the trouble with having a large family (there are five princes and princesses now. I really think they should stop). Osborne is nearly finished and, if you like Italian villas by the English seaside, it would be the sort of thing you'd like. Personally, I find the Horn Room a little creepy. Every single thing in it is made of antlers, from the chairs and tables to the chandelier. What on earth would a deer think, if it looked through the windows?

'Oh dear, oh dear!!'

Buckingham Palace is being altered too. They're adding a balcony at the front, for waving to crowds, and a wing at the back, for guests, balls, dinner parties and I don't know what else. I doubt they'll do anything about the servants' quarters.

I have been summoned to the Lord Chamberlain's office. I'm either going to get dismissed or promoted. Fingers crossed.

## Autumn 1846
## Buckingham Palace

Ma'am (rhymes with smarm) is what we personal maids call QV when we chat with her face to face. I'd call her the Empress of Pingpong if that's what I had to do to keep this job. I've moved out of the laundry, hoorah! Away from the mangles and the endless buckets of washing soda, and upstairs to the Royal wardrobe, where I fluff up the Royal petticoats. Here I am, stitching silk ribbons on to the undergarments of the woman who rules over an Empire on which the sun never sets. I'm the first person she sees in the morning and the last person she sees at night, (apart from Albert, of course) so I shall make it my business to be sure she's ruling the world properly.

Here's my diagram of the Empire. It makes you proud to be British, although I sometimes wonder if the peoples of India and Africa feel quite the same way about British Dominion. I must mention this to Smarm.

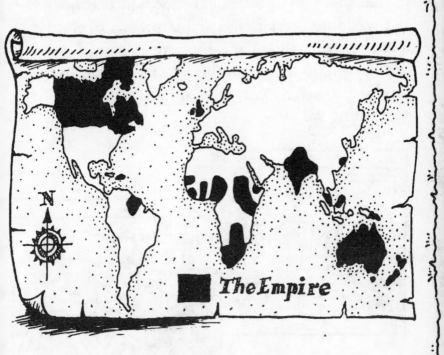

We have a new Prime Minister, called Lord John Russell. He seems like a nice chap and he wants to do something (but not too much) for poor people. But he is so very, very short. Even Ma'am calls him a 'little man' and who is she to talk?

## June 1847
## Osborne House

William and I got married last week. Mrs Flora Porter, that's me! Ma'am gave me a little brooch as a wedding present and William got a tiepin. I was choked. William and Flora does have a certain ring to it, not unlike Victoria and Albert. I'm busy stitching entwined initials onto everything we own.

## 31st July, 1847

Ma'am and I went for a sea bath yesterday. Our first. We drove down to the beach in a horse and cart and then the Queen entered her bathing machine. Inside, she changed into her bathing costume, then she stepped out on to the curtained veranda of the bathing machine, walked down some steps to the sea and began plunging about like a porpoise. Once the sea had modestly covered her body, we pulled the bathing machine away. What a performance. I just jumped in and splashed about. I think sea bathing is wonderful, but it would be better if you didn't have to wear bulky costumes with stockings and a hat.

## Spring 1848
## Buckingham Palace

Speaking of inventions, here's something that might just catch on. It's called a photograph and it's something to do with light, a piece of glass, a pewter plate and a big black box. It takes pictures of people who sit in front of it (as long as they stand still for about an hour). Just imagine if you could take pictures that moved! And talked!

Just when you thought it was all right to be royal, something crops up to change your mind. Apparently, people all over Europe are revolting against royal families and that's making Ma'am very nervous. The French king and his family arrived at Buckingham Palace in tatters and moved in without a by-your-leave. I feel sorry for the laundry maids. There are rumours of it happening here, so Ma'am's come up with a decree ordering her ladies to go to balls wearing British dresses made from British silk. Presumably she wants to humour the loonies from the silk stocking industry, in case they come up with any more fancy ideas for dressing Albert in short petticoats.

## Autumn 1848
## Balmoral

Sir and Smarm are looking for another private hideaway. Well you can see why. Buckingham Palace, Windsor Castle, Osborne House... I mean three castles just aren't enough. So we're in Scotland where Smarm has found 'a pretty little Castle in the old Scotch style'.

She has also decided that everyone has to wear kilts, except herself, of course. She can wear a proper dress made from tartan! The wee children have all been trussed up in Highland gear and Albert (according to William) had such difficulties with the belts and buckles of his tartan skirt (sorry, kilt) that it made him late for dinner. Smarm is very happy playing at being an ordinary person. She even asked me to look out some of her old petticoats so that she could hand them round to the crofters' wives. She goes out fishing with Albert and on long horseback rides with the highland servants, or ghillies as they call them up here. Her favourite ghillie is a cheeky, bearded fellow called John Brown. Och ay the noo.

*Autumn 1849*
*Balmoral.*

Beat *hop*! Beat *hop*! One two three *hop*!  A beat, and *down* and *turn* and *hop!* That's Scottish dancing for you, and we are all at it. Well, Ma'am and the kids are and I've been roped in too. It has to be said, Ma'am is not exactly light on her feet, but the dancing master is very polite about her efforts.

Ma'am is besotted with anything Scottish, so it is haggis, neeps and porridge all round. She has taken to sending Albert off for a day's shooting and stalking with a packed lunch, just like the ghillies take. Only QV gets Albert's packed in a silver box so no-one will ever forget he's a *prince*.

Someone's just invented the safety pin. What with Ma'am's constantly expanding waistline, it could save me a lot of sewing.

*Spring 1851*
*Buckingham Palace*

Prince Albert has been busy again. He has organised a Great Exhibition to celebrate art, inventions and general worldwide ingenuity. It started as an idea to celebrate work and peace. I suppose he felt he had to do something after all those revolting peasants in Europe gave them such a fright. All the stands and exhibits are under the most enormous glass dome in Hyde Park, called the Crystal Palace. It makes you proud to be British.

But nothing is ever as straightforward as it seems, is it?

• Ma'am is very nervous about the glass building because last year a hailstorm shattered every glass roof at the Palace, and it took ages to clear up.

• The public are in a tizzy because they think the foreign exhibitors will bring the plague.

• The politicians are in a state because they think the foreign exhibitors will bring revolution and cheap foreign goods that will put the silk stocking weavers out of business, and they might all be forced to wear short trousers and petticoats.

• The kings and queens of Europe won't come, for various reasons. Some of them think the glass ceiling will fall on their heads, and some think they will be shot by revolting peasants in petticoats.

• Birds have roosted in the trees inside the dome, and see no reason to leave. They are probably looking forward to covering the exhibits with their droppings.

• Some numbskull had planned to fire off a gun salute to open the exhibition. The Prime Minister had to explain to him gently that a gun salute could shatter the crystal dome into a million slivers of glass.

I think Albert is a saint dealing with that lot.

Here are some of the best things from the Exhibition:

The sewing machine. You just push the fabric along and a needle and thread stabs up and down and does the sewing for you.

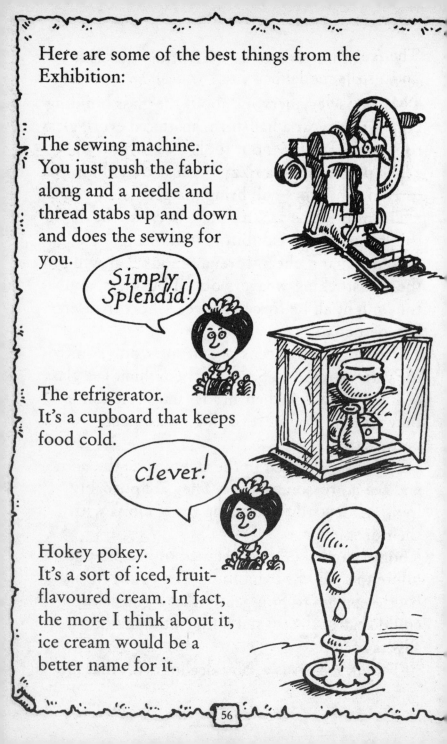

*Simply Splendid!*

The refrigerator. It's a cupboard that keeps food cold.

*Clever!*

Hokey pokey. It's a sort of iced, fruit-flavoured cream. In fact, the more I think about it, ice cream would be a better name for it.

The American stand has a display of handguns and a scale model of a huge waterfall called the Niagara Falls.

One of the German stands has a tableau of tiny stuffed frogs dressed up as people.

I was amazed to discover that you can send a message in Morse code down the electric telegraph wires and they can pick up the blips and bleeps at the other end straight away! They'll be sending people to the moon next, I shouldn't wonder.

## Autumn 1851

The Great Exhibition was a *great* success. Millions of people came from all over the world and the show actually made a thumping profit. Albert has started building a museum in South Kensington with the money. And guess what? He's going to call it the Victoria and Albert Museum. Ma'am is beside herself with pride and delight at her beloved husband's success. She thinks people might stop thinking he's a German prince and start thinking of him as an English king. Some hope!

## Spring 1852

We've got another new Prime Minister called Lord Derby. Ma'am doesn't think much of him and Albert thinks he's altogether too fast and racy. He won't last.

## February 1853

I wasn't wrong. By December of last year, the Earl of Aberdeen got the top job. Ma'am thinks he's a dear, so that's all right.

The latest bit of excitement is that the dining room at Windsor burst into flames. QV and her ladies sat and watched the servants running about rescuing furniture and sloshing water all over the place from the safety of the Green Drawing Room. Albert squelched back and forth between the firefighters and his beloved reporting on progress and issuing orders. Needless to say Albert now wants to re-build Windsor so it will never burst into flames again.

# Spring 1853

Another royal baby! More washing! Prince Leopold made his entrance into the world on the 7th April and made medical history. Ma'am was given chloroform to ease the pain of childbirth, and she pronounced the experience delightful beyond measure. Of course, all the old churchmen are rattling their jowls saying women were born to suffer childbirth because it says so in the Bible, but I think if men had to bear children, Adam would have done a deal with God to invent chloroform first.

William was not at all interested in the chloroform story. He read me out an article from the paper about a mad inventor called George Caley, who has built a kite that can carry people. He calls his invention 'a glider'. Sir George strapped his coachman into the device and sent him soaring up and over the Yorkshire Dales. The coachman resigned the minute he landed, saying he had been hired to drive, not to fly!

## 28th March, 1854

Oh dear. There's a war on. Russia and Turkey are arguing over territory. Britain and France have decided to weigh in on the Turkish side because of some old alliance. Ma'am is furious with the Tsar of Russia, and everyone seems cross with Albert because he is related to the Russian royal family in some remote way. A lot of young men have gone off to fight for something they're not quite sure about in a place they've never heard of. I must look up the Crimea on a map. The Secretary of War has assured Ma'am that all the soldiers have plenty of flannel shirts, drawers and fur caps. He didn't mention guns or bullets. How do you fight a war with a pair of drawers, I'd like to know?

The war is not going well, in spite of the fact that Ma'am is knitting mittens. The troops are starving and dying of cholera. Foolish generals are ordering mounted soldiers with swords to charge cannons. *Into the Valley of Death* as Lord Tennyson puts it so poetically. Everyone's blaming the Prime Minister for the war, so 'dear' Aberdeen is out and Palmerston is in. He's seventy-one, deaf and blind. His false teeth fall out when he talks, but he does what Ma'am says, and she likes that in a Prime Minister.

## Summer 1855

William and I strolled over to Hyde Park Corner last Sunday – it was a brilliant sunny morning. We wandered over to where a crowd had gathered. Standing on a wooden box was a man rabbitting on about high food prices and low wages. I looked over my shoulder to see if a troop of Mr Peel's policemen were coming to march him off to the deepest dungeon, but no such luck! The boring old so-and-so ranted on all afternoon, sending everyone to sleep. This is called 'Free Speech' apparently, and it means anyone can say what they like (except about the royals, that's called treason). Pity, really. I could sell juicy titbits of palace gossip at a penny a go and make a fortune.

## Autumn 1856

Ma'am has take a shine to Florence Nightingale, the nursing 'angel' who seems to me the only person who was at all sensible in the Crimean War. She went out there with nurses, blankets, bandages and medicine. Florence came to the Palace for dinner to talk about her experiences and the result is that Ma'am has became mad about hospital visiting. She bustles around the wards dispensing smiles and encouraging words to the wounded men. She'd be digging out the bullets herself, given half a chance.

Just in case any one thinks I'm taking life easy being a wardrobe maid, may I just remind you what the fashionable lady wears under her clothes these days:

A linen chemise, a corset, a corset cover, stockings, garters, drawers, a bustle pad to give skirts a fashionable bump at the back, waist petticoats (various), a full length petticoat with a stiffened hem and extra red flannel petticoats in the winter. Albert, on the other hand, only has to struggle into a shirt and loose cotton drawers, and perhaps a corset for special occasions, to improve his posture and waistline.

Bustles are *the* thing, at the moment, but the proper ones, which are stuffed with horsehair, are quite expensive. I read a story about a lady out walking in Chester who was wearing a bustle pad stuffed with bran. To her great surprise, she was savaged by a hungry donkey. The lengths we women go to for fashion! I find a bundle of kitchen dusters does the job admirably.

## Autumn 1851

News is filtering through from America about a certain Mrs Amelia Bloomer, who has an outrageous idea that women should wear shorter skirts over baggy trousers called, needless to say, Bloomers! The very idea is making the ladies at the Palace *blush*! I mean, ladies aren't supposed to have legs, they just have long skirts that glide along and nobody even wants to think about what goes on between the waist and the sole of a shoe.

## Spring 1855

Speaking of fashionable things, the rage now is to replace twenty layers of petticoats with a crinoline frame made of wire hoops. Ma'am disapproves of them, of course, and will stick to her petticoats. We have had some fun, though. Ladies have been falling out of carriages and getting stuck in doorways and a lady falling over wearing a crinoline generally exposes a lot more than she decently should.

A lady-in-waiting tripped up at a State reception in Paris in front of King Victor Emmanuel. She was wearing open drawers, like every lady should, and by all accounts the King was absolutely delighted with the view.

However, our own dear Duchess of Manchester caused no end of alarm when she tipped head over heels climbing a stile. Apparently, everyone (including the gentlemen in

the party) were treated to a
view of her scarlet tartan
knickerbockers.
Disgusting!

Knickerbockers
are a racy invention
named after cartoon
characters called 'the
Knickerbockers' – a
Dutch-American
family who are drawn
wearing loose breeches
fastened at the knee.
Toffee-nosed gents have rather
taken to wearing tweedy knickerbockers as they
stride about the moors shooting birds, but for a
woman to wear such things is frankly shocking!
Whatever next!

Here's an invention that could
really make a difference to the
world: The inflatable crinoline –
it only needs a small
foot pump!

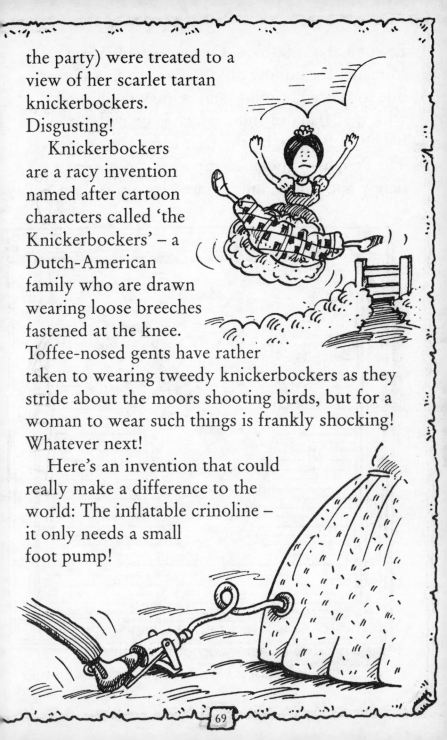

Enough about fashion. Our esteemed Prime Minister, the doddery old Palmerston, is a great one for Foreign Policy and is busying himself with the affairs of India which is owned, on behalf of Britain, by the East India Company. The People of India are apparently not very happy about it and may start a revolt.

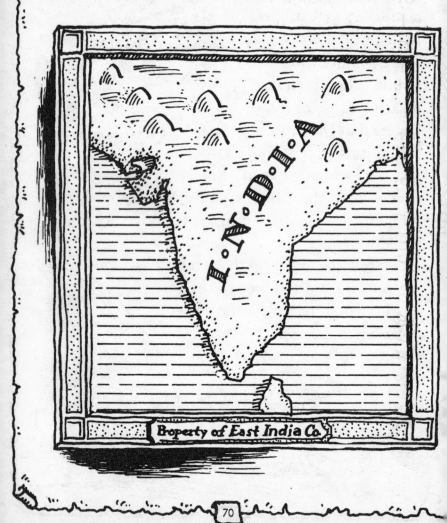

I·N·D·I·A

Property of East India Co.

# Spring 1857

Another royal baby. Nine children is enough for anyone, and Ma'am gets very ratty when she's pregnant. She's actually put me off having children. She pushed and pushed the Princess Royal (her eldest daughter, Vicky) to get engaged to Fritz, the Crown Prince of Prussia, who's a perfectly nice young man, but now Ma'am is getting all weepy at the thought of her beloved Vicky going off to live in Prussia. I mean what does QV want? Everyone's a bit confused and there's a lot of tip-toeing around the Palace trying not to say the wrong thing or wake the baby.

If you ask me, Albert is looking extremely unwell. He's putting on weight, he's rheumaticky, nearly bald and off his food. Maybe it's because he's worried about Bertie, the Prince of Wales. He has every right to be worried. The boy's stupid, lazy and distinctly sulky. It's a great shame Princess Vicky can't be heir to the throne – she's clever, pretty and kind.

Why does it always have to be the First Boy, especially when this particular first boy's such a failure?

## 25 June, 1857

This might help Albert feel better. Ma'am has managed to make him Prince Consort. This means he's not Prince Albert of Saxe-Coburg any longer and he doesn't have to wait in line with other assorted European princes when they all get together for a party. Basically, it means he can now sit next to his wife.

## February 1858

The Princess Royal's wedding was a great success. The Palace has been full of short, fat German relations and a lot of sharp-looking young princes with moustaches, who smile at the ladies and click their heels.

William and I have been worked off our feet, as usual, what with all the balls and banquets and endless changes of clothes, but everything is quiet now. The young couple have set off for Prussia. Ma'am has dried her eyes and has started writing to Vicky every day, sometimes twice a day.

## Summer 1858

This has been the year of The Great Stink. It has been so unbearably hot this summer that the River Thames, into which everyone unloads the contents of their chamber pots, is surging with bugs, flies and worse. The Smell will go down in history.

The brand new Houses of Parliament are nearing completion on a magnificent site by the river. Needless to say, there's a slight problem here. The stench from the river is so pungent, that they've had to put up blinds sprayed with bleach so that members of Parliament can go about their business without pegs on their noses.

## Spring 1861

General gloom has descended over the Palace.
- The Queen's mother has died, and it's thrown Ma'am into a complete fit of the vapours. She became close to the old Duchess over the years and was devastated to discover how much her mother had loved her, in spite of all the awful things they said to each other in the past.
- The new royal doctor has been killed in a train crash.
- The Portuguese royal family have been carried off by typhoid.
- Bertie has been caught in the company of some young actress, just when he's supposed to be persuading Princess Alexandra of Denmark that he'd make a delightful and faithful husband.

Things can't get much worse.

*December 1861*

Oh yes they can. Prince Albert is dead.

I have never seen anyone as distraught as poor old Ma'am. I have to keep reminding myself that we're the same age – she's turned into a pudgy mound of despair and it's impossible to find words to comfort her.

I'm being kept busy, though. Her entire wardrobe has to turn black. The whole country has been plunged into mourning. Even the railings outside people's houses have been painted black and there isn't a yard of black fabric left in the whole of London.

## February 1862

We have all retreated to Osborne so that Ma'am can weep in peace. Meanwhile, Albert's clothes are laid out for him every day as if he were still alive and William has to take his (empty) chamber pot for cleaning every morning and replace it ceremoniously in his commode every evening. Ma'am sleeps clutching his night shirt. This is not healthy.

On a somewhat happier note, teams of young men are now being paid to play football and William spends every spare minute checking up on the results of the games in the newspaper. His favourite team is Notts County. When they win, he leaps up and down like a madman waving Albert's potty and shrieking *Up the Magpies!* He is a hooligan!

## Autumn 1862

Oh Lord! Will she ever stop weeping? Poor Princess Alice (number three child) got married in July and it was more like a funeral than a wedding. Ma'am's mad for memorials. The Blue Room, where Albert died, has been turned into a shrine, she's commissioned a thumping great memorial for Hyde Park (with a statue of Albert clutching the catalogue of the Great Exhibition) and she's moving her beloved's corpse to the mausoleum she's just had built at Frogmore in the grounds of Windsor Castle. Statues, busts and portraits of Albert are popping up all over the place.

## Spring 1863

Bertie finally succeeded with Princess Alexandra of Denmark. She's very pretty and sweet and I don't think he deserves her. It was a lovely wedding, but the Queen of Gloom never smiled, just gazed like a sick cow at a bust of Albert. When will she snap out of it? She's completely lost interest in her job. I'd like to help out but are the British people ready for the State opening of Parliament to be conducted by a wardrobe maid? Actually, they could do a whole lot worse – I think I'd be *excellent*.

It's so gloomy at the Castle that William and I like to get out and about as much as we can. London has a new underground railway that we call the 'Drain' but the company who built it like to call it the Metropolitan Line. I must say, I thought it would be as dark as a dungeon and as smelly as a sewer – full of rats and decomposing corpses. However, I was wrong. You get on a neat little gas-lit steam train and get whisked underneath London at a rattling speed.

Someone's invented roller skates, and about time too. Watching William skidding around with little wheels strapped to his feet, gave me such a good laugh I almost feel I can face old Gloomy Guts and her wardrobe full of widow's weeds. Why can't the fat little woman pull herself together?

## Spring 1864

It would appear that I'm not the only one to notice that Ma'am is taking this mourning a little too seriously. Some pranksters have stuck posters on the gates of Buckingham Palace.

These
Commanding
Premises
TO BE LET OR SOLD
IN CONSEQUENCE
OF THE LATE OCCUPANTS
DECLINING
Business

Ma'am just looked even more miserable when she heard about it and got herself a note from the royal doctor to say she was too sick to appear in public.

Meanwhile, Bertie and his Princess are dashing all over the place, making themselves very popular.

That might get Ma'am moving, one thing she hates is competition. She's getting rattled at the thought that her daughter will one day be Empress of Germany, leaving Ma'am a plain old Queen. She'd like to find somewhere to be Empress of, that's for sure.

I don't know if this has been the wisest thing Ma'am has ever done, but it has certainly cheered her up. She has sent for John Brown, her favourite ghillie, to come down from Balmoral and be her permanent personal attendant! It's all very odd, if you ask me. He's bravely 'saved' her from countless carriage and horse-riding accidents that she never seemed to have before. He treats her as if she were... well an ordinary woman rather than the Queen of Just About Everywhere. He says things to her like "Hoots, then, wumman". I mean, she'd kill anyone else who dared be so cheeky. "But he's so handy with shawls and cloaks", says Ma'am. "Mmmm" say I.

we are amused!

Hoots then wumman.

## Summer 1865
## Osborne House

We've decamped to Osborne House for the summer to get away from the summertime stink. It comes as no surprise that John Brown's come too.

Mrs Brown, as people are beginning to call Ma'am, is quite under his spell and all the stuffy old courtiers are up in arms about it. Who knows what JB and Ma'am get up to when they set off on their little expeditions? I shall make it my business to find out.

## Winter 1865
## Buckingham Palace

Prime Ministers come and go and then come back again. I know that when you are compiling a diary for posterity, it is your duty to record all these things – so here goes.

Palmerston has just died from the strain of dealing with a mutiny in India, and cleverly sitting on the fence while the northern and southern states of America were at each other's throats, so we've got little Lord Russell again. Ma'am never liked either of them, the 'two dreadful old men', she called them. Now it's one down and one to go.

## 1868

Well, Russell can't handle it, so Lord Derby's had a go and now we've got Mr Disraeli. Ma'am looks like the cat that's got the cream. Mr Disraeli begs for 'the benefit of your Majesty's guidance' and appears to consult her about everything. Who knows if he takes a blind bit of notice of her, but she loves it. I must say, she does take this ruling business quite seriously.

## Winter 1869

Never mind the politics. Some Frenchman has just wasted his entire life inventing Margarine, something that's supposed to be better for you than butter, but tastes revolting. It might be good for Ma'am's figure though!

Ma'am's definitely perked up a bit, what with the competition from her children *and* the John Brown 'affair', although she still looks like a little tub of lard. It's almost back to normal: dinner parties with seven courses, followed by entertainments of all kinds (does anyone ever think of the poor staff?) But as far as Ma'am's wardrobe goes, it's always the same dizzy choice between black, black or black.

## Summer 1870

Oh can't you just smell the difference? London's sewer system is now complete and it's almost a pleasure to walk by the Thames.

# Spring 1872

Just when the Royals had sunk to the lowest possible position in the popularity polls, and an MP called Sir Charles Dilke was rattling on about getting rid of the Royals and setting up a Republic, everything changed. Bertie nearly died of typhoid and a Mr O'Connor took a pot-shot at Ma'am. There's nothing like a bout of misfortune to make people like you again, so now she's Queen Popular.

PM-wise, she's struggling a bit with Mr Gladstone after enjoying the devotion of Mr Disraeli. Gladstone is an incomprehensible old windbag who speaks in sentences that ramble on into the middle of next week.

## Spring 1876

Ma'am got her Mr Disraeli back and guess what he's done for her now? He's managed to make her Empress of India, so she's as pleased as punch and thinks the sun shines out of Disraeli's bottom.

## Summer 1876
## Balmoral

I'd just been thinking that there must to be a better way to communicate than hurrying up and down stairs and corridors carrying sealed-up notes on silver trays, when I read in the *The Times* that Alexander Graham Bell, a gentleman who lives in America, has patented a device called the tele-phone. Apparently, all you need is a speaking tube and a listening horn and a wire. The sounds of the voice are turned into pulses, sent down the wire and then turned back into speech at the other end!

Why did no one think of it before? If you can tele-phone from one room to another, soon it will be from one house to another, and then what? It'll be tele-vision next, mark my words!

How on earth will I keep track of what everyone's up to if they start tele-phoning each other? This morning, for instance, I took yet another note from Ma'am to JB and wild horses wouldn't drag the contents from me. Actually, she was, as usual, setting up a meeting with 'her dearest John' in the hunting lodge.

Must hasten to the hunting lodge to gather evidence for posterity.

Well, she's a funny old thing, is Ma'am. Some people think she and JB hike off to the hunting lodge for a wee spot of high jinks, but it's not like that at all. This is what I saw, peering through the shutters.

First, she fussed about and made him take off his wet socks and she warmed them in front of the fire, while she made tea and they settled back and passed the time of day like an old married couple. I sometimes think she'd like to swap places with William and me – well for a while anyway. I don't think she'd like to live on our wages.

# Autumn 1877

Mr Edison from America has invented the phonograph. It's an instrument that records the human voice. This will change the world, just you wait. Mr Gladstone had a go at recording one of his interminably boring speeches but I'd be surprised if anyone other than his mother bought a copy. I think Mr Edison could make a fortune if he signed up some really popular band to play for his phonograph. Everyone would want a recording then.

## Summer 1879
## Balmoral

The older William and I get, the more astonished we are at the way things are changing. The Butler types up menus and notices on a typewriter now; people who can afford it go on holidays abroad; lady missionaries are setting out for Africa; some American women can vote; Mr Darwin thinks we are all descended from apes and... only the *seriously* unfashionable wear crinolines.

Here at Balmoral, a legion of plumbers have gone mad installing bathrooms like you've never seen in your life before with water closets that flush and baths that are filled by hot water taps. I'm not so sure about the new sewage systems, though. I just hope they can cope with all this flushing.

## 1879

There is a war on in Africa. Ma'am is an absolute sucker for brave, young, dark-skinned warriors. So much so that when Zulu warriors hacked the Prince Imperial to death, (the son of one of her best friends, no less) she claimed to be 'delighted' to hear that they had 'mercifully' severed the arteries in his neck so he would die instantly, and had sewn up the cuts in his uniform. Make that merciful, neat, brave, young, dark-skinned warriors.

Speaking of sewing, the fashion now is for closed drawers with the inside seams stitched up! They are called knickerbocker-drawers and are considered very racy. Combinations are a new rage, they are basically a chemise and drawers combined and are far less bulky to wear. Men wear them, too. William and I are both fans of combinations, even though we're getting a bit old to be trying out new fashions.

## 1883

I've neglected my diary of late, because I don't seem to have the energy I used to. Ma'am is holding up quite well considering that Disraeli's gone and, worse still, John Brown died this year. Needless to say, she's got all the monument builders in Britain hard at it again making statues and endless plaques to her beloved John. She's taking an interest in the utterly dismal lives of the poor and is wondering out loud if they have a grudge against the upper classes. I suspect she only does it to annoy Mr Gladstone – he is apparently so weary of battling with Ma'am that he's had to go on a cruise. Ah me! What it is to have money and status.

Things are hotting up again in Africa, people are revolting in Egypt and further south in the Sudan. Mr Gladstone wants to get the British troops out, but Ma'am wants to keep them in. So they've sent General Gordon to sort things out. Ma'am thinks Gordon is the bees knees, but actually he's got a mad glint in his eyes and apparently he's already asking for reinforcements. As William so wisely pointed out, why do you need reinforcements to take British troops *out*?

In America they have built an exciting new building called a 'skyscraper'. The Home Insurance Building in Chicago has an a iron frame and it rises ten storeys high! How fortunate, therefore, that a certain Mr Otis has already invented the elevator.

William was right about General Gordon, of course. He went out with no intention of bringing back the British troops. He went there to act the hero and has ended up skewered with native spears.

This has been the year of the Queen's Golden Jubilee, which means she's been sitting on that throne for fifty years. All over the Empire (she likes it when you say that) prisoners are being released in her honour, ghastly poems are being composed and endless congratulatory telegrams are cluttering up the Palace postroom. The Queen was so exhausted by all this that she fled to the South of France for a holiday. And why not?

I've ruled for 50 years

When the day finally dawned, there was another great row. Everyone expected the Queen to wear a crown for the service at Westminster Abbey. Oh no! Ma'am obstinately wore her widow's bonnet with a couple of diamonds stuck to it. I will say she did make an effort for the banquet that night, and she got herself done up in a brilliant sparkly dress.

Somehow, in the course of all the present-giving, she has acquired two Indian servants. One of them is nothing to write home about, but the other, Abdul Karim, is twenty-four, slim, dark-skinned, tall and clever. Needless to say, Ma'am is completely dazzled by him, and has started taking Hindustani lessons and eating curry.

## Spring 1888

This has been a very sad year for me. I must have mentioned that my William is an absolute number one fan of Nottingham County Football Club. Well, this year the Football Association organised the first ever football league season in which twelve teams all play each other and one team gets to be top of the League and the others don't. Well, William had been jumping up and down yelling 'Up the Magpies!' for weeks on end, presumably hoping that the Magpies would somehow be encouraged by his shouts and play a little better. When Preston won the cup and his beloved Magpies came second to bottom, William took to his bed and within a week he was dead. The doctor said he died of disappointment.

## Winter 1888

Now that I'm getting old, I spend more time in my rocking chair in front of the fire reading the paper. I have to say that I don't think it's doing me much good. The sordid details of Jack the Ripper's murderous reign of terror give me the collywobbles, but the story has gripped everyone's imagination and no-one can talk of anything else. Five victims so far, all women, all horribly mutilated.

Apparently Scotland Yard is heaving with detectives rushing about with bits of bloodstained clothing and magnifying glasses. But they are getting nowhere, which is odd. The gossip columns are beginning to speculate that Someone, Somewhere doesn't want the murderer found. Some people say the Ripper is rich and well-connected, with friends in very high places. Ma'am is terribly upset about the whole thing and keeps pestering her ministers for updates on the investigation. She's begun asking Bertie to account for his actions. I wonder…??? NO! The boy's overweight and a bit of a pompous bore. And certainly all this hanging around, twiddling his thumbs while waiting to be King has done nothing for his temper, but he's no crazed serial killer. All the same…

## 1889
## Hampton Court

Like the Queen, I am getting old and
rheumaticky. Ma'am has kindly given me rooms
at Hampton Court Palace and a pension for my
retirement. I was driven out to Hampton Court
by a cheeky young footman in a motor car, an
amazing horseless carriage with a mind of its
own. Luckily, someone
walked in front of us
all the way waving a
red flag.

I shall miss
being at the centre
of things, but life
approaching the
turn of the century is
so full of surprises that
I'm sure I'll find plenty to
fill my days. Ma'am is now busy marrying off
her grandchildren, which is quite a difficult job as
they're all related to one another. If someone
doesn't keep track of what's going on, they'll
start interbreeding and producing imbeciles.
What those royal princesses need is a few
strapping young footmen.

## 1897

The years roll by, and I find I have abandoned my diary. But an invitation to celebrate the Queen's Diamond Jubilee – that's sixty years on the throne – demands an entry. Ma'am gets wheeled about in a chair now, just like me. We had a touching reunion in a corridor at Buckingham Palace which I felt I should record for the nation.

> Ah Flora, where are my black bombazine petticoats?

> I haven't been near your drawers for ten years, Ma'am.

> We are not amused.

Actually, Ma'am and I did have a bit of a gossip after all the balls and dinners were over and done with. I said I'd had a lovely time, but as everyone I knew was dead, I'd had no-one to share it with which was a bit sad. She said she felt just the same way, but she had to soldier on for the good of the Nation.

She asked me what I thought had been the most amazing developments over the past ten years, and I said the invention of the toothpaste tube, the radio, moving pictures and a breakfast cereal called Shredded Wheat. She, on the other hand, rated a general improvement of morals, with women having more accomplishments, men drinking less and dogs behaving better towards the furniture. I couldn't think of anything to say about that, but there was no stopping her. She rambled on about the general high regard for the British monarchy in spite of people revolting all over Europe and the abysmal record of her predecessors: the Madman, the Filthy Letch and the Silly-arse. She had a point there, of course, but just at that moment Bertie strode by with a lady who was not his wife, and I remember thinking to myself: "I wonder how long before one of them blows all her hard work out of the water."

## January 22nd, 1901

Queen Victoria died peacefully this evening at six-thirty. The news made me feel very sad and old. She was a funny woman – not funny ha-ha, but funny peculiar. One minute she was all girlish enthusiasm, the next she was stamping her feet in a rage. One minute she was stern and shocked, the next she was flirting outrageously with dark-skinned warriors. The truth is, she was just human, she didn't ask to be Queen, and underneath that crown she was just like me, really.

I feel very tired as I write this, and ready to go and join my William. It's just my luck. After a lifetime of toil in service, someone's now invented the vacuum cleaner.

# HISTORICAL NOTE
## by Professor Dullas Ditchwater, Eminent Historian

My lawyers are dealing with Ms Parsons' allegations that my tomes on Queen Victoria are 'extremely dusty'. Her outrageous suggestion that I am in the habit of throwing litter from my window is the subject of an on-going libel action and is therefore *subjudice*.

I now turn to my real reason for dismissing the so-called diaries of the never-before-heard-of Flora McTavish as being 'idle tittle-tattle' and 'worthless gossip'. I dismissed them, for a very good reason: *There is absolutely no proof of the existence of Flora McTavish. Nor of Brian, Stanley, William or any of the other young men that kept catching her fancy, the flighty little so-and-so.*

It is true that in this so-called 'Lost Diary' the events and main characters are accurately portrayed. But in the books that I write, accuracy is always backed up by vast numbers of dates and footnotes, which every student of history knows are good for you. *The Lost Diary of Queen Victoria's Undermaid* is backed up with silly drawings and far too many jokes. My ten-volume work on Queen Victoria may be largely unread by the general public, but it is the definitive work of this monarch and has no mention of underpants. My mother said she found Volume One 'immensely interesting'. So there.

Edward

Alfred

Victoria

Alice

# ND ALBERT

Helena

Arthur

Beatrice

Louise

Leopold

# PRIME MINISTERS ...

**Lord Melbourne 1779 – 1848**

*Prime Minister in 1834, then from 1835 – 41*

Queen Victoria's first Prime Minister, her first trusted adviser and the pe
who taught her all about politics.

**Sir Robert Peel 1788 – 1850**

*Prime Minister from 1834 – 5, then again from 1841 – 6*

Created the police force in 1829 while Home Secretary.
Pushed through a Factory Act limiting the working hours of
women and children. Introduced income tax. Generally considered
one of the founding fathers of the modern Conservative Party.

**Lord John Russell 1792 – 1878**

*Prime Minister from 1846 – 52, then again from 1865 – 6.*

Tried to help the poor with another Factory Act to further
limit working hours.

**Earl of Derby 1799 – 1869**

*Prime Minister in 1852, then again from 1858 – 9
and yet again from 1866 – 8.*

Introduced the India Act, transferring the government of India
from the East India Company to the Crown. Gave the vote
to farm labourers.

**Earl of Aberdeen 1784 – 1860**

*Prime Minister from 1852 – 5*

Led Britain into the Crimean War against Russia in 1854, but the war was so unpopular with the people that he was forced to resign from office soon after.

**Viscount Palmerston 1784 – 1865**

*Prime Minister from 1855 – 8 and again from 1859 – 65*

Took Hong Kong from China, ended the Crimean War, suppressed a major revolt in India and sat back and watched the American Civil War without taking sides.

**Benjamin Disraeli 1804 – 1881**

*Prime Minister in 1868, then for a longer spell from 1874 – 80.*

Good on domestic reform: instituted Trade Unions, housing for the poor, mains water supplies, rubbish collection and compulsory schooling. On the foreign front, he declared QV Empress of India and bought the Suez Canal with some loose change he found at the Treasury.

**William Ewart Gladstone 1809 – 1898**

*Prime Minister from 1868 – 74, then 1880 – 5, and 1892 – 4*

Strengthened the Education Act and the Trade Union Act, introduced secret voting and 'Time gentlemen, Please!' in public houses. He wanted Home Rule for Ireland and resigned when his Bill was defeated in Parliament.